THE MELTON MOWBRAY
NAVIGATION

by
M. G. MILLER and S.M. FLETCHER

THE
MELTON MOWBRAY
NAVIGATION

M.G. Miller
& S. Fletcher

**RAILWAY AND CANAL
HISTORICAL SOCIETY
1984**

First published 1984 by the Railway & Canal Historical Society

Registered Office: 12 High Street, Oakham, Leicestershire LE15 6AW

ISBN 0 901461 37 7

Typeset by Moorland Publishing Co Ltd, Ashbourne, Derbyshire
Printed by Dotesios (Printers) Ltd, Bradford on Avon, Wiltshire

Preface

The Melton Mowbray Navigation (MMN) by which the rivers Wreak and Eye[1] were made navigable, receives only brief mention in Charles Hadfield's *Canals of the East Midlands*; yet this has been the only readily available source of information about a waterway where, even though closed more than a century ago, substantial remains of the navigation works still exist. This study, originally compiled as part of the requirements for a three year part-time course in Industrial Archaeology, provides a guide, both historical and topographical, for those exploring the Navigation. The detailed field and documentary survey work was carried out in 1978-79 with revision and updating in 1982 for this publication. The field survey was initially stimulated by news that the Severn-Trent Water Authority was planning substantial drainage improvement works on the River which would have affected the remaining Navigation structures. This work commenced in 1982 and will take about seven years to complete.

The authors' work has been stimulated and encouraged by many others who have helped them either directly or indirectly. Dave Goodwin, who had begun researching the Navigation independently, walked the entire distance with an improvised surveyor's wheel to produce a distance table. John Fletcher carried out all the black and white site photography. The Course Tutor, Dr. Marilyn Palmer of Loughborough University provided guidelines for our approach and taught us much about historical research methods, whilst David Palmer provided the equipment and expertise for the survey of levels at the Kirby Bellars lock site. Thanks are also due to Bob Payne who first showed Michael some of the sites in 1976, and who directed our attention to Melton Mowbray items amongst the Leicester Navigation Papers in the County Record Office. Charles Hadfield helped not only through his published work but also by lending us his file of notes on the Navigation. Similarly Guy Hemingway and Gordon Rattenbury, both members of the Railway and Canal Historical Society, provided lists of newspaper and other references. Other R & CHS members, in particular Grahame Boyes and Dennis Hadley, checked the manuscript and provided detailed comment and suggestions. Finally we would like to thank Mr. J. A. Tyldesley, Divisional Engineer of the Severn Trent Water Authority for the information he gave us about the river and the drainage improvement works, Mrs. Kathleen Ward who recognised the origin of the Navigation Company's motto 'Tendimus in Latium', and Pauline Miller who helped with the typing. The photographs of Lewin bridge and Melton Mowbray basin are reproduced with the permission of Leicestershire Museums Service. The maps were redrawn for publication by Christine Warr, and Dennis Hadley edited the manuscript.

History

Regional Background[2]

Although the East Midlands does not spring to mind as an area of major waterway construction it did develop a respectable network of navigable waterways. Over a forty year span at the turn of the 18th century 210 miles of canal and river navigation were constructed in the area bounded by Cromford, Derby, Grantham, Oakham and Leicester, a not insignificant contribution to the 4500 mile total of British waterways. Apart from the Cromford Canal with its major aqueducts at Lea Wood and Ambergate and the 3063 yard tunnel at Butterley, the region's topography enabled the network to be constructed without heavy engineering works, and hence relatively cheaply.

Waterway development in the East Midlands reflected the national pattern of growth, beginning with river improvement. In 1699 the Trent, naturally navigable to Wilden Ferry, was improved for a further 19 miles to Burton. In 1721 the Derwent was made navigable for 10 miles to Derby and in 1778 the Soar was made navigable to Loughborough from its junction with the Trent, a distance of 9 miles. The first canal on the East Midlands scene was the Trent & Mersey, completed in 1777, which skirted Burton, joining the Trent at Derwent Mouth. Two years later the Erewash Canal was constructed from collieries near Langley Mill to the Trent 12 miles away. These five schemes provided a basic network of a through East-West route (Trent & Mersey Canal and Trent Navigation) with North and South spurs providing transport from collieries to several of the main towns — Burton, Derby, Loughborough, Nottingham — and giving access to Gainsborough, an important transhipment point between sea-going and inland vessels. This basic system remained unchanged for 15 years, until the onset of the national 'canal mania' of the early 1790s. During the mania, the early canals and navigations having been seen to be successful (the Loughborough Navigation was paying 20% dividends by 1790, rising to 155% by 1828), a great many waterway schemes were promoted including several in the East Midlands.

In the four years 1794 to 1797, a further 126 miles of waterway came into use in the area, linking the towns of Grantham, Leicester and Melton Mowbray with the national system. Following this burst of activity a few others struggled to completion or partial completion. A canal linked Oakham with the MMN at Melton in 1802, and a southward extension of the Leicester Navigation — the Leicestershire & Northamptonshire Union Canal — reached Market Harborough (in fits and starts) by 1809. This latter canal never reached its projected goal of Northampton but gained a southerly link in 1814 via the Grand Union Canal from Foxton to the Grand Junction Canal near Watford Gap. So ended waterway construction in the East Midlands.

Promoting and Gaining the Act

In order to build a canal or make a river navigable it was necessary to gain an Act of Parliament authorising the setting up of a company, giving it the necessary powers to carry out the work. Gaining an Act was a lengthy business involving petitions, surveys and books of intending subscribers. There was usually controversy between those for and against the navigation and the saga of promotion can often be traced through contemporary newspaper announcements and reports.

Following the commercial success of the Loughborough Navigation and the Erewash Canal in the late 1770s, proposals were made in 1780 for the extension of the navigation up the river Soar to Leicester and the Wreak to Melton[3] but nothing came of these. In 1785 the scheme was revived with public meetings at Nottingham Castle on 28 September, 20 October, and 24 November. Although supported by the Earl of Harborough the proposals were opposed by the Leicestershire colliery owners who feared the water route would enable Derbyshire coal to compete unfairly with their own which was carried overland. However by 29 October the Leicester & Nottingham Journal was able to report that William Jessop was taking a survey of the river 'Reke' (sic) and that £6000 had been subscribed the first day the books were opened. The first meeting in Melton itself was held at the Swan Inn on 16 November to consider the proposals and take subscriptions.[4]

The MMN scheme stimulated other ideas. Consideration was given to making the River Eye navigable from Melton to Oakham and for cutting a canal from Melton to Stamford.[5] The former eventually came to fruition as the Oakham Canal completed in 1802, but the latter was never built.

Meanwhile, at a meeting in November, obviously to placate the Leicestershire coal owners, it was resolved that a navigation from Coleorton to Loughborough would be of general advantage. Debate continued, however. A letter signed 'Pro Patria' supported the navigation schemes as they would provide cheap coal for the growing industry, whilst another, signed 'A freeholder to the County of Leicester and a friend to the Navigation' suggests that the Almighty had provided a nearly level river for human advantage, supporting his arguments with biblical references to the carriage of goods by water. Varying estimates of the likely trade on the Soar and Wreak were put forward suggesting likely returns on capital of 10%, $3\frac{3}{4}$% and 6 or 7%. Others sought to capitalize on the public interest; 'Now engraving and speedily will be published, a view of the intending navigations in this county now under consideration..'[6]

By December the survey plan was ready for inspection and a petition to Parliament supporting the proposal was ready for signing. In January 1786, 'a numerous meeting' at the Swan Inn, Melton resolved to apply to Parliament 'for leave to bring in a petition to open the river'. In February, John Noble having been appointed treasurer, a 5% call was made on subscriptions to cover the costs incurred, and the clauses of the intending Bill were being considered.[7]

At this stage it was decided to divide the scheme into two, and petitions for separate Bills were presented to the House of Commons in early March. One was for making the Soar navigable from Loughborough to Leicester with a branch canal to Thringstone Bridge near Coleorton i.e. similar to the Leicester Navigation and Charnwood Forest branch as finally constructed. The other was for making the Soar navigable to its junction with the Wreak, the Wreak itself being made navigable to Melton Mowbray. The section from Loughborough to the Soar-Wreak junction was common to both, presumably in the hope that even if the Leicester scheme was defeated the MMN could still proceed.[8]

The Bills were read for the first time on 7 and 13 April respectively but when the Leicester Bill came up for its second reading on 9 May it was defeated by 51 votes to 42. Opposition from powerful landowners, millowners and the mortgagees of the Burleigh Bridge-Ashby de la Zouch Turnpike had overcome the petitions of other landholders, the Corporation of Leicester, and the inhabitants of Market Harborough, Kettering, Oakham, and Stamford. The last three also petitioned in favour of the Melton Mowbray Bill, mentioning the proposals for the extension of the navigation to their towns, but without success, the Bill being effectively shelved by the House's vote to postpone its second reading for three months.[9]

Debate about the merits and demerits of the navigation proposals and suggestions for renewed attempts to obtain Bills continued throughout the next few years but did not reach the stage of petitioning Parliament until 1789. On 9 February of that year a public meeting took place at the Black Swan in Melton at which it was resolved to open a subscription in order to apply again to Parliament. This time the two schemes were combined and a petition for a single Bill — for making the Soar navigable from Loughborough to Leicester and the Wreak to Melton Mowbray — was presented to the House of Commons on 18 March 1789. Petitions in support came not only from the Corporation of Leicester and the inhabitants of Market Harborough, Kettering, Stamford, Uppingham and Oakham but also from as far afield as Worcester, Cheshire (salt works proprietors) and Hull (merchants and shipowners).[10]

The promoters had, however, made the mistake of omitting the Coleorton branch thereby attracting the opposition of the Leicestershire coal proprietors and their road carriers, together with that of the land and mill owners and of the Loughborough Navigation Company who feared that additional locks on the Soar would obstruct their water supply. Thus all the effort and enthusiasm of the promoters came to naught when their Bill was defeated by 73 votes to 35 at its second reading on 14 May.[11]

However the idea was not long dormant. Meetings were held the following year, 1790, to further consider 'a general plan of navigation in the county of Leicester' and to resolve any disagreements with those who had opposed the previous Bill. Once again the proposal was divided into two separate schemes, the MMN Bill being limited to making the Wreak navigable to Melton Mowbray, the Soar and Charnwood Forest line being left to the Leicester Navigation Bill. By now the main objectors to the Leicester scheme had been won over and opposing petitions were presented only by certain turnpike interests and the proprietors of the Leicester coal weighing machine. Accordingly the Leicester Navigation Act duly received the Royal Assent on 13 May 1791.[12]

Meanwhile the Melton Mowbray Bill, to which there was no opposition, was making rapid progress following the presentation of its petition on 11 February, and its first reading in March. In five working days, 17-23 May, it passed through the Commons third reading, the Lords' first and second reading, Committee stage and third reading. And at long last, on 6 June 1791, finally gained the Royal Assent, a decade after the proposal had first been made to put Melton Mowbray on the waterway map.[13]

The Act

The Act[14] itself is a good source for the intentions of the promoters. Its date of commencement is 5th July 1791 and the 75 printed pages give detailed information about the route, proprietors, general and special provisions of construction, authorised capital, toll rates, rights and obligations of millers, and means of settling disputes. The Act incorporated the 'Company of Proprietors of the Navigation from the Leicester Navigation to Melton Mowbray, in the County of Leicester 'with powers to make the rivers Wreak and Eye navigable for the carriage of coal, stone, lime, limestone, timber, lead, and all kinds of merchandize' from a junction with the Leicester Navigation near 'Turnwater Meadow in the Lordship of Cossington to Mill Close Homestead, in the parish of Melton Mowbray'.

Seven titled proprietors are named: the Dukes of Rutland and Newcastle, the Earls of Winchelsea and Harborough and Earl Ferrers, Lord Middleton and Lord Viscount Melbourne. Some of these names are associated with other local waterways. The Duke of Rutland and Lord Middleton, for example were also main promoters of the Grantham Canal. The 79 other proprietors of the MMN include Christopher Staveley (surveyor, and then resident engineer), Charles Latham senior (father to Charles junior, a solicitor who became Clerk to the Company) and Col. John Frewen Turner of Cold Overton Hall (who served on the committees of both the MMN and the Oakham Canal).

The Company was given powers to acquire land for making artificial cuts; this was not to exceed 20 yards width except at basins and turning places where it could be up to 50 yards. The towing path was not to exceed 3 yards width on straight sections or 6 yards on crooked lengths. No buildings were to be erected or wharf set up on Play Close or Causey Hill Close (both part of Lord Melbourne's lands) nor on Bridge Leys, Ormonds Piece or Prior's Close (lands of William Reeve).

Authorised share capital was £25,000 (250 shares of £100) with an extra £5000 if necessary either by subscription amongst the shareholders or by loans on mortgage of the tolls — but further supplementary sources were to be needed before the Navigation was completed. As was common at the time, 5% interest was to be paid whilst work was in progress. There were to be two general meetings annually, the first to be at 'the house of Francis Ward, known by the sign of the White Swan in Melton Mowbray aforesaid, upon the first Wednesday after the commencement of this Act'. The Committee was to consist of between 9 and 13 members to be elected annually in July, and was to meet at least once a month. Share calls were not to be for more than 10% at a time, nor more frequently than one every two months.

Maximum tonnage rates were typical of the time with coal at 2/6d per ton from the junction to Eye Kettleby, Sysonby or Melton, or $2\frac{1}{2}$d per ton mile to other destinations. 'Iron, timber and other goods wares and merchandizes' were to be charged 4/-d for the through journey or 4d per ton mile, with building materials and roadstone at half the rate for coal. 'Dung soil, marle, ashes of coal and turf, and other manure', would be carried free if for use on land adjoining the Navigation, and provided that water was topping the weirs. Riparian landowners or tenants could use pleasure boats freely if locks were not passed.

The Act thus not only spelled out the Company's powers directly relevant to constructing and running the Navigation but also protected the rights and privileges of neighbouring landowners. Indeed the route itself was in part determined to accommodate the wishes of important landowners. The Leicester Navigation, for example, made use of the bottom mile of the river Wreak, this deviation from the Soar being to keep the Navigation further from Wanlip Hall, then owned by Sir Charles Hudson.[15]

As with many other navigations in the East Midlands, William Jessop had been employed as surveyor. He had first surveyed the Wreak, assisted by Christopher Staveley junior, in 1785. It was Staveley who prepared the plan of the MMN deposited with the 1791 Bill, both he and Jessop appearing for it in Parliament.[16] This later plan of the MMN shows more detail than the earlier one for the combined Soar and Wreak schemes. Plot numbers are shown, referring to a schedule of landowners, and a red line denotes the towpath. Proposals for the lock sites and for straightening awkward curves are indicated, the results of the latter surviving on modern maps and on the ground, where cut off loops are in many cases still very clear.

The ten existing mill sites on the river determined the locations of the locks, and the height of the mill weirs governed the rise of each lock. Where the mill was still in use the miller's rights to water had to be preserved, and the map shows how the lock cuts were planned at each site. Higher up the valley, where the river becomes narrower, the lock cuts are longer. In every case the lock is shown positioned at the upper end of the cut, but Jessop's work on the Thames led him to change these plans and the locks were actually built at the lower end. Jessop wrote of improving navigation on the Thames, '...a tail cut from a lock on river navigations should be as short as possible, because after floods the eddy that is formed at the entrance into the river is generally the cause of a bar ... which is most easily to be removed by drawing the sluices of the lock...'[17] It is also clear that to dig a long shallow head cut and a short deep tail cut involves less excavation, and is therefore cheaper than digging a short head cut and a long tail cut.

Construction

Whilst the promotion of the Melton Mowbray Navigation is fully reported in contemporary newspapers, its construction and operation get less coverage. To make matters worse the company papers have not survived and neither the Waterway Museum nor the Public Record Office hold any records of the Navigation. Consequently the researcher has to rely on finding occasional chance snippets of information from other sources.

As its motto the Company adopted a phrase from Virgil 'tendimus in latium' (Aeneid I, 205). In translation the full sentence reads, 'Through diverse misfortune, through so many crises, we are making for Latium where destiny reveals quiet abodes.' A fanciful choice, but not inapt, even though, compared with many schemes arising during the 'canal mania', the MMN's construction was reasonably straightforward. Charles Latham junior was appointed Clerk with Joseph Noble as Treasurer and, following the initial meeting, invitations to contractors were put out in the Nottingham and Leicester Journals.[18]

Simultaneously a 5% call was made to subscribers.[19] The Share Register[20] shows a typical mix of shareholders. Apart from the titled and various 'gentlemen' and 'esquires', they were mostly local professional people — 'Doctor of Physic', 'Doctor in Divinity' — plus tradesmen and farmers — butchers, bakers, brewers, brushmakers, carpenters, drapers, hosiers, matchmakers, millers, a cheese factor, carriers, woolcombers and graziers — and a few widows and spinsters. Apart from the proprietors mentioned in the Act, names of others with waterway interests appear, such as John Varley, surveyor to the Leicester Navigation, and John Pinkerton, the contractor who was involved with the Sussex Ouse Navigation and several canals including the Barnsley, the Gloucester & Berkeley, and Basingstoke. Although addresses range as far afield as Leeds, Kent and Bristol, most subscribers were local. Share transactions were frequent at first but gradually fell off to less than 12 a year by 1835 and 3 a year by 1860.[21]

Fund raising continued with further calls to a total of £25 per share by April 1792. Such frequent calls might have dampened enthusiasm, yet others were eager to join the subscribers as evidenced by advertisements seeking to buy shares in the Navigation. The national canal mania was now approaching its height with many new schemes being proposed, including extensions of the MMN to Oakham and the Leicester Navigation to Northampton via Market

Harborough. By the end of 1792 there was a desperate scramble to get hold of any canal shares. An auction in Leicester saw high prices being paid: 642 guineas for one share in the Erewash Canal, 765 guineas for one in the Loughborough Navigation, and 175 for one in the Leicester Company but only 84 for a share in the MMN.[22]

Meanwhile the Company seems to have been pressing on with the work. In December 1792 they advertised in the Lincoln & Stamford Mercury: 'Wanted on the Melton Navigation, several brickmakers to engage for the coming season. Also bricklayers and carpenters who have been used to Navigation works. Apply to Christopher Staveley Jnr.' Eighteen months later the same journal reveals further progress. 'Committee will meet 6 June (1794) at Blackmoor's Head, Melton to contract for building and finishing two locks, one at Thrussington Mill, the other, at Kerby (sic), the Company to find bricks, the contractor all other materials'. On the 7 November the paper announced: 'In a few days, the Melton Canal will be open to Melton Mowbray' but this was premature (perhaps a misunderstanding?) as the next day the Nottingham Journal reported the Navigation open only to Frisby Mill.[23]

The work was apparently costing more than estimated, not uncommon during the inflation caused by the Napoleonic Wars, for on 27 March 1795 the Leicester Journal announced a special general meeting 'to consider how to raise £2500, required beyond £120 on each share already advanced to make the Navigation in that state, as to bring the boats to Melton'.[24] The meeting agreed to raise the money 'for making and completing the Navigation' by making an immediate call of £10 on each share.[25] But there were other indications that all was not well. Christopher Staveley, who had sold his shares in June 1793[26], was 'voted out' on 15 July 1795, according to the diary of Col. John Frewen Turner, a committee member. The same source suggests he was replaced as engineer by William Green, a Nottingham man associated with the Grantham Canal. On 13 August 1795 Green inspected the line with Turner and pronounced both materials and workmanship very bad.[27] However, all the difficulties must have been overcome as the canal appears to have been opened throughout by 1797,[28] although a second act was needed in 1800 to tidy up the Company's debts.[29]

This second Act was described as being to enable the Company 'to complete their Navigation, and to discharge the Debts contracted by them in the making thereof'. It goes on to tell how the original £25,000 plus £5,000 had been spent 'together with all the tolls and duties they have received since the opening of the said navigation, amounting to the further sum of £7,000 and upwards, but have contracted debts to the amount of upwards of £4,000; and some parts of their works are still incomplete'. The Act authorised the raising of a further £10,000 making the total cost about £45,000 for constructing the 14¾ miles of the Navigation with its twelve broad locks.[30] Apparently it was opened without ceremony, as no mention of this has been found in contemporary newspapers, the only direct evidence being the Tonnage Accounts of the Leicester Navigation.

Operation

In the light of the increased expenditure on construction the second Act also authorised the Company to increase the maximum tonnage rates by an additional 1s 0d per ton (or 1d per ton-mile) for coal and 1s 6d (or 1½d per ton-mile) for iron, timber etc; these supplementary tolls were, however, halved for through traffic passing upstream onto the Oakham Canal. The actual tolls charged were amended from time to time in the light of commercial considerations. These changes in tonnage rates can be picked up from newspaper announcements:

> *Derby Mercury*, 25 Jan. 1798: 'Tolls to be reduced. Cokes (Unmixed with coal) slates, tiles and flooring bricks to be 2/6 per ton. Common bricks and raw plaster 1/6 per ton'.

> *Lincoln & Stamford Mercury*, 13 Jan. 1804: 'Melton Canal tonnages to be reduced from 4/-d to 3/-d per ton'.

> *Nottingham Journal*, 5 Sept. 1812: 'Tolls reduced to 3/6 per ton for the whole line of the Melton Navigation and 3½d per ton for shorter distances'.

> *Nottingham Journal*, 18 Sept. 1824: 'At a Special General Meeting 1 August resolved that tonnage on grain entering from the Oakham Canal, and other grain passing along the Melton Canal, shall be reduced by half' — to enable them to compete for traffic with the Grantham and Stamford Canals.

The first references to boats for use on the Navigation appear even before it was fully open. On 31 January 1794 the following advertisement appeared in the Leicester Journal: 'Richard Braithwaite, ship and boat builder will build boats suitable for Leicester or other canals, 30 to 50 tons burthen, not drawing more than 3½ feet when loaded, and with sufficient freeboard for navigation. Either clink or carvel bottoms. Apply to R. Braithwaite, Granby Street, Leicester'.[31] The 1795 *Registry of boats, barges, etc. on Inland Canals and Navigations* lists five 'boats' of '40 tons burthen' operating 'from Melton Mowbray ... to the Erewash and Cromford Canals': each carried a master and two crew, 'one to assist in steering the vessel and the other to drive the horses'. By comparison 37 boats are registered as trading between Leicester and Cromford and 6 between Leicester and Gainsborough.[32]

In 1798 there is another reference in the Leicester Journal: 'To be sold by auction. Two capital Boats with rigging etc. complete for the coal trade built by Barnsdall of Loughborough Dock, one only two years past, and the other but one. In good repair capable of carrying very heavy burthens. Well calculated for the Gainsborough or any Inland Navigation (with wide locks) having worked upon the Grantham, Melton and Union lines ...'.[33] Further information comes from a set of Trent Navigation boat gauging tables published in two volumes in 1799 and 1800. Of the 290 boats included only one is described as trading to Melton. By comparison, amongst 392 other mentions of destination, Leicester occurs 108 times, Loughborough 63 and Grantham 34. Coal is the most popular cargo, being mentioned for 245 out of the 290 boats, then in descending order, corn 46, malt 10, lime 9, limestone 3, timber 3, and slate 3 times.[34] Another glimpse of traffic is given by the frequency of services. In 1830 for example the fly boat services from Birmingham included 6 boats per week serving Melton Mowbray, the same number as Grantham, but 9 to Loughborough and Market Harborough, 12 to Burton, 15 to Derby, 18 to Leicester and no fewer than 20 to Shardlow and 24 to Nottingham.[35]

Little seemed to disturb the Navigation's operation apart from the occasional mishap — 'Wreake and Eye Humane Society. Thanks to Mr Williamson of Gadesby rescued Wm Hudson from the water at Brooksby Lock' — or the inevitable maintenance work — it was closed for 10 weeks in 1820 'on account of the building of Lewin Bridge'; and in 1824 we read, 'Melton Mowbray Navigation wants a steady and active carpenter, preferably one used to canal works'.[36]

Although not amongst the busiest waterways the MMN nevertheless gained a respectable level of waterborne trade, cargoes including not only coal but also wool, lime, granite, wheat, oats, barley and manure from Leicester stables. Tonnage records are incomplete but in 1797 about a fifth of the 78,617 tons carried on the Leicester Navigation — 16,781 tons of coal and 200 tons of wool plus other goods — proceeded onto the MMN. Interestingly, whilst 12,934 tons of coal went up the Navigation, 3,847 tons came down it. No coal occurs near the waterway so presumbly the back carriage was of coal previously carried up to wharves on the MMN being brought down for resale when prices rose in the Leicester market.[37]

Encouraged by the 1791 Act for the MMN the Oakham Canal was successfully promoted, gaining its own Act in 1793. William Jessop had carried out the general survey of the $15\frac{1}{4}$ mile route which, rising through 19 broad locks, would enable boats to proceed from the MMN's terminal basin at Burton Road, past the villages of Saxby, Stapleford, Market Overton and Cottesmore to Oakham. Work began under Christopher Staveley junior, who had carried out the detailed survey, but he was replaced late in 1797 by William Dunn from Sheffield. Like the MMN, the Oakham Canal also ran short of money and had to seek a second Act in 1800 to raise further capital. The line was eventually reported completed in June 1802 at a total cost of £65,000, although, probably because of water supply problems, boats do not appear to have reached Oakham until early in 1803.[38]

The Oakham Canal served an area even more quietly rural than that of the MMN, even though both towns were of similar size (in 1801 Melton's census population was 1730 and Oakham's 1630). Coal went up and agricultural produce came down but never in sufficient quantities to make for financial success. However the Canal did generate much extra traffic for the MMN, about half of whose upward coal trade went on to the Oakham Canal.[39] A printed statement of coal landed on the MMN between 1 January 1839 and 1 January 1842 shows the relative importance of the various wharves. Average annual tonnages were:

14

Syston	64	Hoby	15
Lewin Bridge	495	Frisby	40
Ratcliffe	74	Asfordby	135
Rearsby Wharf	2784	Kirby	27
Thrussington	620	Melton	6287
Brooksby	261		

Such records provide the only evidence for some wharves on the navigation; for others there is documentary evidence, though not all can be identified on the ground. Syston mill had a wharf, for in 1816 there was a law-suit concerning damage caused to the private mill road that gave access to the wharf.[40]

Rearsby wharf was established in the early days of the navigation by the Kilby family, who retained their interest in the site for sixty years. The wharf, at the end of an artificial cut, was used to bring in coal for distribution to the villages of eastern Leicestershire, and for loading timber.

When the Brooksby Hall estate was sold in 1850 the property was described as including a wharf, though its site has not been identified. Asfordby had a basin close to the village centre in Brook Lane, lying off the river channel at some distance from the navigation.[41]

In Melton Mowbray a series of wharves served the navigation over the years. In 1808 there was a wharf at Priors Close west of the basin.[42] By 1836 the wharfage had extended to include a new warehouse, a granary, malt offices and a coal yard,[43] together with a short arm at right angles to the canal.[44]

Of the wharf sites only Rearsby, Asfordby and Melton Mowbray offer any physical evidence, though some supposition as to sites can be made at Lewin Bridge and Thrussington.

As trade built up so the MMN Company's financial situation improved. In 1804 it was announced in the Leicester Journal that 'Money advanced by Proprietors above £120 per share will be paid off with interest and dividend of £2:8s:0d per share made on the original capital'.[45] As the concern prospered so dividends rose: 1809 $7\frac{1}{2}$%, 1813 6%, 1821 10%, 1833 10%, 1838 10%. By the late 1830s the Company was collecting over £4,000 in tolls each year, and the future must have seemed secure, but there were ominous puffs of smoke over the horizon.

The Coming of the Railway, Decline and Closure

During the early 1840s the Oakham Canal, which had never paid dividends higher than £5 per £130 share, was only able to keep its trade in competition with the Grantham and Stamford Canals by reducing tolls. It was thus in a precarious position when proposals were made for the construction of a railway between Syston and Stamford (later Syston and Peterborough). On 11 October 1844 'George Hudson himself came to Oakham to announce that plans were to be deposited and that the Midland would meet the canal shareholders on amicable terms'.[46] The dry summer of 1844 had not helped as the canal had been closed for lack of water for five months. Consequently on 19 April 1845 the canal company agreed to sell itself to the Midland Railway. The Railway Act was duly passed as was that for the sale and abandonment of the canal, the sale being completed on 29 October 1847.[47]

The railway followed the Wreak valley and in places the river and the Navigation had to be diverted for it. Above Thrussington lock the apex of a bend was straightened and above Brooksby a large loop was cut off, shortening the Navigation by about a tenth of a mile. The railway crossed the Navigation twice below Washstones Ford lock but without altering the line of the waterway, whilst at Kirby Bellars a loop of river was cut off and a new channel excavated, the lock cut being unaffected.[48]

Although the railway caused little physical change to the MMN it had a disastrous effect on its commercial position. In the year to 31 March 1845 the Oakham Canal had carried 31,182 tons of goods, two thirds of this being coal carried upwards. The closure of the canal meant this trade was lost to the Melton Navigation and the opening of the railway from Syston to Melton on 1 September 1846 and to Oakham on 1 May 1848 (it ran partly over the bed of the dry canal) reduced traffic even further. The effects are clearly reflected in the Company's annual accounts:[49]

| | | Includes these items proceeding to Oakham Canal | | | |
Year ending	Total Tonnage	Coal	Coke	Merchandise	Total
1 July 1845	53640	25177	110	4102	29389
1846	57099	25315	-	5863	31178
1847	68896	31371	-	8080	39451
1848	30879	1740	-	327	2067
1849	18031	-	-	-	-
1850	13301	-	-	-	-
1851	17087	-	-	-	-

In order to keep some traffic from the railway toll rates were reduced within a year to a fifth of their previous level i.e. to 6d per ton for the whole distance. As a result toll revenue fell even more sharply. Whereas £4830 13s 6d had been collected for the year to 1 July 1847, this fell to £1440 15s 3d for 1847/48 and to £415 11s 4d for 1848/49. Desperately the Company sought to cut expenditure. In a letter circulated by William Latham, the Clerk, and dated 5 July 1848 the resolutions taken at the annual general meeting are listed. As well as toll reductions and a nil dividend they include:

That David Staniforth, the Company's Surveyor, be removed from his present residence at Hoby to the Melton Wharf, and that he there undertake and perform the duties of Wharfinger, as well as his present duties of Surveyor.
That Three Months' Notice be given to William Sprigg, the Wharfinger at Melton, to quit his situation, the Company hereby testifying to his excellent

character and conduct while in their service, and regretting being necessitated to dismiss him.

That the Salary of Mr. Johnson, the Pay Clerk and General Superintendent, be reduced from Thirty to Twenty Pounds per annum.[50]

The amount spent on repairs was also reduced. Whereas £703 had been spent for the year to mid 1845 and £887 to mid 1846, it was cut to £485 in 1846/47, to £363 in 1847/48 and to £191 in 1848/49. But it was no use. The Company's financial situation continued its inexorable decline, as reflected in the dividends declared. Whereas £14 had been paid for each £120 share in 1847 it was nil in 1848 and 1849 resuming with a mere 15s 0d for the second half of 1850. Annual amounts thereafter never exceeded £1 2s 0d finally declining from 15s 0d in 1861 to 5s 0d — less than $\frac{1}{4}$% — in 1869.

Closure became inevitable. In 1862 the MMN had offered itself to the Loughborough Navigation but they declined to buy, as did the Midland Railway. The doomed Navigation lingered on with little trade and no hope, and in 1877, after a final offer to the Midland Railway which was once again rebuffed, applied for an Act of abandonment. Even this did not go unopposed, a petition being presented in the House of Lords in 1877 by twelve 'landowners, riparian owners and wharf owner'.[51] In it the petitioners claim they use the Navigation for bringing large quantities of 'coal, lime and manure and other materials from Leicester and other places' both for their own use and others. It also expresses concern about flooding once the Navigation is unsupervised, and that the future bill for the repair of bridges, roads and culverts would fall upon themselves as ratepayers. However the resistance was only a token and the Melton Mowbray Navigation (Abandonment) Act which authorised the closure to take effect from 1 August 1877, was duly passed.[52] All that remained was to wind up the affairs of the Company.[53]

To meet the concerns of the riparian landowners the Act included clauses requiring the company to repair or rebuild all structures before abandoning them and for lock gates to be replaced by weirs of the same height as the existing river weirs. Accordingly an independent engineer, A. W. Dalton, was commissioned to prepare a survey of works required. This he did with the help of James Cuspley, engineer to the Leicester Navigation Company. In his report Dalton suggests that all the bridges and locks could be put in good order for £855. On bridges he writes:

> The present inconvenient approaches having been made to suit the requirements of the canal traffic, when that traffic ceases the company should lower such approaches to the satisfaction of the users of such bridges ... or give compensation for same.[54]

Accordingly at Rearsby Mill the bridge was given a flat cast-iron deck on the original bridge abutments and at Kirby Bellars the canal bridge was completely rebuilt.

Dalton had given estimates for repairing the lock gates but instead, as required by the Act, the gates were removed and weirs constructed above the upper cills. Built of brick and stone on a crescent plan, and springing from the upper gate quoins, these regulated water levels. A pencil sketch on the cover of the copy of the Act of Abandonment in the Leicestershire County Record Office shows a plan of such a weir.[55] Dalton also suggested that maintenance should be provided for the embankments at Asfordby Wharf and alongside the Ratcliffe/Rearsby road. Land occupied by towpaths, which was rented rather than owned by the MMN, reverted to landowners.

Conclusion

For a waterway serving an agricultural region with relatively sparse population the MMN had not done too badly. Even though costing almost twice its estimate, at £3100 per mile it had still been cheap to build. The MMN depended for its revenue mainly on coal brought up for domestic sale, plus building materials and a small back trade in grain. To have achieved, under these circumstances, a peak trade of more than 60,000 tons a year, and paid dividends up to $11\frac{1}{2}\%$ was very satisfactory, particularly as it did not form part of an important through route.

Once the railway came, closing the Oakham Canal and also competing directly with the MMN, the Navigation's fate was sealed. It managed to cling on for another 30 years, and even after closure occasionally carried local traffic: a photograph dated c. 1933 shows sacks of grain being loaded onto a punt at Rearsby Mill for transport to Ratcliffe[56] and in 1979 a dilapidated pleasure cruiser was moored on the outskirts of Melton.

Today, a century after closure, the physical remains are still there to be seen but their decay and disappearance will be hastened by the Water Authority's drainage improvement. The plans propose generally lowering water levels by widening and regrading, the removal of weirs at Syston Mills, Ratcliffe Meadow Lock and Ratcliffe Mill, the construction of new weirs at Rearsby and Thrussington Mills and the demolition of Brooksby lock chamber.[57] However the valley is still secluded, the main roads mostly keeping well clear of the river. Walking beside the old Navigation it is easy to dream of restoration, and of once more being able to approach Melton Mowbray by water.

The Melton Mowbray Navigation Today

The towpath of the MMN is no longer a public right of way throughout, so many features are more easily visited by car or by using cross-valley footpaths. Ordnance Survey 1:50,000 map, sheet 129, or 1:25,000 sheets SK 61 and SK 71 cover the route.

Junction to Syston Mill Lock (0.0-0.5 miles)

The MMN left the Grand Union Canal (Leicester Section) at Turnwater Meadow, between Rothley and Syston (SK 608122), and used the improved River Wreake for $14\frac{1}{2}$ miles north-east to Melton Mowbray. Southwards the Leicester Section takes an artificial cut for about 2 miles, but west of the Junction for $1\frac{1}{2}$ miles to Cossington lock it uses the improved course of the Wreake, so a short section of the river is still navigable.

From the junction a public right of way follows the old towpath on the left bank of the river. Just upstream of the modern concrete footbridge carrying the GUC towpath over the river the piers of an earlier towpath bridge can be seen beneath the water. Soon a small stream enters the river on the offside. Above the modern bridge carrying the A46 trunk road the first of the double-arched bridges on the MMN is reached. The bridge, built to carry the footpath between Cossington and Syston, has foundations of Mountsorre lgranite blocks, dressed on one face but of irregular shapes and sizes. Both upstream and downstream ends of the central pier are pointed. The upper part of the bridge is of brick, and the arches are two bricks thick, laid in English bond. The bricks that show through the concrete rendering of the parapet are a different size from those of the arches, and probably represent a later repair. The navigation arch — the left-hand arch with the towpath beneath — gave headroom of about 10 feet at normal navigation level.

Just below Syston Mill, on the left bank, is the dry channel of an old river loop, bypassed for ease of navigation; on the right bank the mill stream from Syston Mill enters the river. Syston Mill lock (SK 615125), rise 7ft,[58] has b en rebuilt by the Severn Trent Water Authority to serve a water gauging station, and nothing can be seen of the original structure.

Syston Mill Lock to Ratcliffe Meadow Lock (0.5-1.7 miles)

The towpath was on the left bank over this section, though the modern right

Syston double-arched bridge.

of way (very overgrown) follows it only as far as Lewin bridge, from where it cuts straight across the fields to Ratcliffe Meadow lock.

Just above Syston Mill lock the river is crossed by the Leicester to Nottingham railway line, whose original arched bridge was later widened. The present Lewin bridge carrying the Fosse Way over the river was built in 1956, replacing the earlier structure of 1820. The reinforced wall on the left bank below the bridge may indicate the site of a wharf.

Ratcliffe Meadow lock (SK 627132), or Frog Island as it is known locally, has a rise of only 2ft 6in and was built not at a mill site but at the point where the Queniborough Brook joins the river on the right bank. The brick-lined chamber, which has bullnosed brick copings and dressed stone quoins, is in reasonably sound condition, and clearly visible are such features as hollow quoins, upper cill and culverts, and recesses for the paddle gear within the lower gate recesses. The masonry cill can be seen beneath the later crescent weir at the head of the lock. The lock's overall dimensions are 91ft 10in from heelpost to heelpost, and 14ft 9in wide. Jessop's drawings give the measurements thus: 'length from centre to centre of the gate heels 90ft, width 14ft 6in'.[59] These measurements vary by a few inches on the locks of the MMN, but all were built to allow passage of a boat of 70ft by 14ft 6in.[60]

Lewin bridge, built 1820; prior to demolition 1956.

Ratcliffe Meadow Lock to Ratcliffe Mill Lock (1.7-2.4 miles)

The public footpath follows the route of the towpath on the left bank of the river through meadowland and trees to the site of Ratcliffe Mill lock (SK 631142), where the rise was 5ft 10in. The lock, on private land, has recently been filled in and one wall demolished, and the site is now hidden from view behind a high fence.

Ratcliffe Mill Lock to Rearsby Mill Lock (2.4-3.5 miles)

Immediately above Ratcliffe Mill lock the towpath crossed to the right bank. There is no public right of way close to the river on this section, but some features can be seen from the B674. The milepost, now in the grounds of Newarke Houses Museum, Leicester, but once situated just above the mill weir at SK 632142, bears the legend 'To Junction $2\frac{1}{2}$ miles / To Melton 12 miles, Wilson & Co 1819'. On the left bank is an old wood and brick boathouse with a pantiled roof.

At SK 636142 an artificial cut leaves the river, visible as a shallow depression amid the trees alongside the B674 it is still partially in water. At the bend in the road the cut once continued into the field, but has been infilled. There was a basin at SK 639141, with a scatter of bricks indicating the site of a wharf building. Between here and Rearsby Mill are two cut-off river loops, and a small stream joins from each side just below Rearsby Mill

Milepost Ratcliffe mill.

and lock. The bridge over the lower end of the lock cut has a flat cast-iron deck fitted on to an earlier brick base.

A public right of way passes through the Rearsby Mill complex, but the lock (SK 642149) is on private land belonging to the mill house. The lock, with a rise of 5ft 7in, is unique on the MMN in having steps on each side below the lower gates; nowhere else was the boatman given easy access to his boat when working through the lock. Trees flourish in the silted lock chamber and in its tail cut. Earth has been washed away from behind the right-hand side of the lock chamber to reveal three of the brick land-ties supporting its brickwork. Such land-ties are shown on Jessop's plans, and are intended to hold the wall back against the earth surrounding the chamber. Jessop said: '... the counterforts, which merely are intended as land-ties, should not be built on the bottom, but be set on by steps on the slope of the lock pits, so as to lean against the earth and counteract its lateral pressure; for the wall will never fall backwards: and this construction with much less materials than are otherwise necessary will ensure it from leaning forwards.'[61]

At the upper end of the lock both the crescent weir and the original wooden and brick cill — with bolts protruding from it — are visible above water level. There is an iron ring fixed into the brickwork in the left-hand lower gate recess. This is the only such ring seen on the navigation, and its function has not been ascertained.

Land-tie, Rearsby mill lock.

Crescent weir and cill, Rearsby mill lock.

Rearsby Mill Lock to Thrussington Mill Lock (3.5-4.9 miles)

The towpath was on the right-hand side between these two locks, but today there is no public right of way close to the river. Between Rearsby Mill lock and Thrussington village there are two cut-off loops. On the left bank below Thrussington double-arched bridge is a long levelled area about twenty feet wide, said locally to be the site of the village wharf.

Just below Thrussington Mill lock the Ox Brook enters from the left. The lock site is approached via a public footpath from Rearsby, but the lock itself lies in private ground belonging to the mill house.

A single-arch footbridge crosses the river on to the lock island near the tail of the lock. This bridge has a stone base, with a brick arch which may be original although the parapets are modern.

Of Thrussington Mill lock (SK 657157), which had a rise of 6ft 3in, the right-hand wall no longer exists. Some of its stones have been used to build a path near the old mill building, now a store. Several brick piers, probably the land-ties of the demolished wall, are visible amongst the scrub. The left-hand wall with its bullnosed brick coping is in good condition, and behind it the ground has fallen away to reveal three land-ties, closer together than those at Rearsby. The upper gate recess has been partly obscured by a modern footbridge, but a paddle gear recess is visible. At the tail of the lock the coping, unlike that of the other locks, slopes downwards at the gate recess. The lock has lost its cills. In addition to the river weir there is a spill weir 10 feet wide across the upper end of the lock island.

Thrussington Mill Lock to Brooksby Lock (4.9-6.0 miles)

Along this stretch of the river much straightening was required to make it navigable, and three of the cut-off loops can be seen today. Further straightening became necessary when the railway was built close to the river just above Thrussington Mill lock.

The towpath, at first on the right bank, changed to the left bank at a turnover bridge (SK 663162), used by a right of way from Thrussington village to Brooksby. The single arch of this gated bridge is now cracked and flattened. Only the brick abutments remain of the bridge which once carried the towpath on to the lock island.

At Brooksby lock (SK 669164), rise 7ft 7in, the river normally flows through the chamber and only uses its original channel when water levels are high. As a result of frequent flooding Brooksby lock is in the worst condition of any on the MMN and will be demolished by the Severn Trent - Water Authority.[62] The poor state of the lock chamber enables us to see some of the details of its construction. Nothing remains of the upper cill or the upstream half of the right-hand wall, and a large bay has been scoured out. The left-hand wall with its bullnosed brick coping is complete in its length but the facings on both sides have fallen away, revealing that the inside bricks are all headers and that the wall is held together by metal straps. Behind the left-hand wall two land-ties are exposed, about three feet square and 13ft apart. The stones from the upper right-hand quoin, including two with anchor strap recesses, are dumped in the field by the lock. Just above the lock on the left-hand side are the remains of a weir, at nearly 120 feet the longest on the navigation.

Brooksby lock during floods.

Brooksby Lock to Hoby Lock (6.0-7.0 miles)

The building of the railway through Brooksby caused a large loop of the navigation to be bypassed, shortening the distance between Brooksby and Hoby locks by about a tenth of a mile. The old channel can be seen on the southern side of the railway.

The towpath lay along the left bank of the river on this section. Today there is a pleasant walk along the public footpath from Rotherby which follows the right bank to Hoby bridge, where it crosses to the left bank until Hoby lock.

Hoby bridge (SK 672169), built of brick on stone foundations, has a single arch, now flattened at the top, with a string course of two rows of bricks, a rounded brick coping and rectangular pillars at each end of the curved parapets — a typical bridge built according to Jessop's plans drawn for the Leicester Navigation. There are no signs of a towpath beneath the bridge although it is wide enough to have accommodated one; there are towrope grooves on the left-hand side of the arch.

Hoby bridge and village.

Water House, Hoby.

The MMN had an office at Hoby, and a chain was fastened across the waterway here to prevent the movement of boats during restricted hours.[63] It seems likely that the Water House, a private residence situated between a cut-off loop and the navigation channel, was the Company office, for no other house in Hoby is near the river. On the bank opposite is the lower part of a once-sturdy wooden post, which may have been used to support the chain across the river.

The tail of Hoby lock (SK 674174), rise 4ft 10in, is crossed by a brick footbridge in a very poor state of repair. The lock chamber, with its bullnosed brick copings, is complete, but its construction has been exposed by erosion behind the chamber walls. The lower right-hand gate anchor strap has left a good impression in the stonework of the quoin, and compares well with the drawing made by Jessop for anchor straps for the Leicester Navigation. This is another detail which suggests that Jessop's designs for the Leicester Navigation were also used on the MMN. No drawings specifically made for the latter have been found.

At the upper end of the lock the crescent weir has collapsed and exposed the original wooden cill, built of five horizontal wooden baulks laid across the lock, with more horizontal baulks behind them laid at an angle of 45°.

Although not identical, this construction bears a strong resemblance to Jessop's drawings for a wooden cill for the Leicester Navigation. A dam of brick and concrete, built at the head of the lock cut, has been breached and a narrow water channel flows through the heavily silted cut.

Hoby Lock to Washstones Lock (7.0-8.4 miles)

The towpath was on the left bank between these two locks, but no public right of way runs near the river today.

Austen Dyke, which has been re-routed, enters on the left bank below the bridge carrying the Syston and Peterborough Railway over the river. The gated road from Rotherby to Washstones crosses the river on a double-arched bridge at SK 683174, then crosses a stream on a miniature double-arched bridge. The river bridge has its arches, string course and cutwater in blue engineering bricks, probably the result of later repair work, but the underneath of the arch is in rough red bricks. There is a towpath nearly six feet wide under the left-hand arch. Just above this bridge on the right bank is a marshy area known as the Wailes, now a nature reserve, which is surrounded by an old river loop.

The cut to Washstones lock is just above the next railway bridge. The lock itself (SK 687179), with a rise of 5ft 2in, was, like Ratcliffe Meadow lock, built where no mill existed. Before Austen Dyke was diverted it would have emptied into the river here, so the lock was sited to bypass an area where silting from the sidestream was a possibility.

The lock, in poor condition, with the facing bricks fallen away, can easily be seen from the road bridge and the adjacent field. Behind the crescent weir at the upper end of the lock the paddle holes are visible, and in front of it is the original masonry and timber cill. The stones of the quoin have ropemarks on them.

Washstones Lock to Frisby Lock (8.4-9.2 miles)

The towpath was on the left bank, but there is no public right of way over this stretch today. Just below Frisby lock are the roughly-dressed stone abutments of a bridge which once carried the towpath across the river.

Frisby lock (SK 698181), rise 6ft 2in, has a single-arched bridge over its tail, with ropemarks both beneath the arch and on the pillar at the end of the parapet. The lock, which is incorporated in the garden of a private house, has been maintained in good condition with a rubble weir at its lower end. Water normally flows through the lock as well as in the river channel. The chamber, of brick with dressed-stone quoins and copings, has the usual crescent weir at the upper end, later lowered by one course of stone. The river weir above the lock, with its wooden footbridge, was destroyed in recent floods, but there are plans to rebuild it to reinstate water levels. On the right-hand bank can be seen the end of the mill leat with its iron guillotine gate. The leat ran beneath the railway line to reach the mill, and again to return to the river.

Frisby lock and bridge.

Frisby Lock to Asfordby Lock (9.2-10.0 miles)

The towpath was on the right bank between these two locks, but today no public right of way runs near the river. Three severed loops shown on the original survey map can be seen on the ground between Frisby and Asfordby. The original intention at Asfordby was to build the lock in or very close to the line of the river, but a different scheme was adopted, and a long cut was built, following the far boundaries of the fields whose owners had already been approached by the Company.

The lock, rise 5ft 9in, is in poor condition, with the coping stones removed and dumped in the adjoining field. A modern road bridge has partially obliterated the lower end of the chamber, but at the upper end the crescent weir and upper quoins are visible. The embankments retaining the long lock cut are clearly defined.

At the bottom of Brook Lane (SK 707189) the road widens to meet the site of Asfordby basin, recently filled in and now overgrown.

Asfordby Lock to Kirby Bellars Lock (10.0-11.6 miles)

Again the towpath was on the right bank, but modern access between the locks has been made difficult by gravel workings. The direct footpath between the end of Asfordby lock cut and Kirby Bellars church has been diverted, but another path follows the left bank of the river from the eastern end of Asfordby village, leading to Kirby Bellars lock. Half way between the locks a brook joins the river on the left bank, and nearby is a pumphouse built some time before 1920 to serve the Holwell Iron Works at Asfordby Hill. Staveley's survey map shows a mill site at Kirby Bellars, but the mill was out of use when the navigation was constructed. Any remains would have been obliterated when the river was straightened for the building of the Syston and Peterborough Railway, although the mill pond is still indicated on the 1:25,000 O.S. map as a depression south of the railway line.

Kirby Bellars lock (SK 719180), with a rise of 6ft 4in, holds water, but the head of the chamber is usually accessible above the crescent weir. Most features can be seen from the footbridge crossing the head of the lock. The left-hand wall of the brick chamber is intact, but the facing layer of the right-hand wall has partly fallen away. In front of the crescent weir the remains of the cill can be seen. The level area of the cill behind the weir proved to be built of bricks and baulks of timber similar to Jessop's alternative plan for cills on the Leicester Navigation. The paddle holes, two feet square, are clearly visible, as is the left-hand blow-hole, about four inches square. At the head of the lock the curtain walls curve away to the full width of the cut as described in Jessop's instructions.

The long lock cut, now dry, has the usual profile, being deep on the outside of the bend and shallow on the inside. Near its upper end a brick bridge with a flat deck and straight parapets carries an ancient right of way. The bridge, which has insufficient headroom for a boat to have passed beneath, is built on older foundations of the familiar Jessop type, and it seems likely that it was rebuilt under the terms of the Act of Abandonment of 1877 in which landowners were given the option of having bridges rebuilt or put into good repair. The bridge certainly existed by 1883, when an Ordnance Survey benchmark was carved on it.

In the river at the corner of the field are the remains of a weir with a working width of 11ft 10in. The level of the water for navigation purposes would need to have been more than five feet above the bed of the weir, but the sluices have been removed sometime after abandonment and the building of the bridge.

River weir, Kirby Bellars.

Kirby Bellars Lock to Eye Kettleby Lock (11.6-12.9 miles)

The towpath was on the left bank between these two locks, but there is no right of way near the river today. About a third of a mile downstream from Eye Kettleby lock a red brick bridge carries the route of the towpath over a stream. Eye Kettleby double-arched bridge (SK 737183), crossed by a public footpath passing through the site of Eye Kettleby mill, has its arches of different sizes, giving it an unbalanced appearance.

Near Eye Kettleby lock are extensive weirs, used to control flooding in Melton Mowbray. The lock (SK 738184) which, with a rise of 8ft 2in, was the deepest on the navigation, has been fitted with metal guillotine gates and sluices at the upper end as part of the flood control scheme. The chamber, which has stone copings, is in good condition, having been repaired with blue engineering bricks.

Eye Kettleby bridge.

Eye Kettleby Lock to Melton Basin (12.9-14.4 miles)

At the upper end of Eye Kettleby lock island are the remains of a footbridge which carried the towpath across to the right bank, which it followed to Melton basin. This is a public right of way and makes a pleasant walk through meadow land and a park to the site of the basin.

Shortly after passing under a multi-arched railway bridge (still in use), the towpath is carried over a small stream. In half a mile a disused railway bridge crosses high over the river. The river channel then continues on the left, whilst the navigation enters an artificial cut forming the boundary of Front Park. The towpath is carried part of the way on the bank formed from the excavated soil of the cut, though some of this bank has now been removed.

Flood control weirs, Eye Kettleby.

Eye Kettleby lock.

Boat inn, Melton Mowbray.

A cast-iron bridge carrying Leicester Road across the cut bears the legend 'Cooke and Sons, Engineers, Melton, 1884'. The Rev. John Ward tells us that at the end of 1884 the new bridge was built and the 'hauling path' beneath it removed, so increasing the width of the road and the flow of the stream. He ascribes the work to a Mr William Clarke, Builder, of Melton, and tells us that it cost around £500.[64] A plan of 1879 shows the old bridge to have been one of Jessop's distinctive style.[65]

Near Melton Mowbray swimming pool a semicircular brick structure can be seen beneath the water on the far bank. The 1879 plan suggests this was the site of stop planks, though the 1904 O.S. 25″ map shows a footbridge here. At this point the cut crosses the river at right angles, and though the section of the channel through Play Close has been filled in, its line is marked by a double row of trees. The final length passes the site of New Wharf where the MMN Company had a warehouse. A concrete wall east of the present building fills the gap left by the short dock and its canopy over the towpath.

Melton Mowbray basin.

Beyond it one wall of the New Wharf building survives, with its loading doorways bricked up.

The basin was situated at the bottom of Burton End, with the Great Dalby road crossing to the west of it over Navigation bridge. The site of the basin has been obliterated by the railway bridge and embankments, but Burton End has changed little during the past century, and the view from the railway bridge is much the same as the view from the basin in an early photograph. East of the basin ran the Oakham Canal, whose wharf site can be seen off Birmingham Row.

The Boat Inn, along Burton End, is now the only reminder of the trade once carried on close by at the basin. Inside are some interesting photographs of old Melton Mowbray, including the basin and Navigation bridge — making it a fitting place to end a visit to the one-time Melton Mowbray Navigation.

References

Preface

1. The river Eye rises on the Jurassic escarpment a few miles north east of Melton Mowbray. Joined by several tributaries, its name changes to Wreake soon after passing through the town. In discussing the history of the Navigation, the earlier spelling 'Wreak' is used, but when describing the physical remains, we use the modern Ordnance Survey spelling 'Wreake'.

    According to the *Concise Oxford Dictionary of Place Names*, the name Wreak is derived from old Scandinavian *vreior*, *'wrathful'*, originally *'twisted'*. E. Ekwall, in *English River Names* (1928) says 'the Wreak is a very winding river and it runs through a strongly Scandinavian district'.

Regional Background

2. This section is derived largely from C. Hadfield: *Canals of the East Midlands*, 2nd ed. David and Charles, 1970, and M.G. Miller: *Waterways of the East Midlands* (unpublished article).

Promoting and Gaining the Act

Note:

LNJ: *Leicester & Nottingham Journal* (divided in 1787 into *Leicester Journal* and *Nottingham Journal*)

LJ: *Leicester Journal*

NJ: *Nottingham Journal*

LSM: *Lincoln & Stamford Mercury*

3. C. Hadfield: *Canals of the East Midlands*, 2nd ed. David and Charles, 1970
4. LNJ 24 Sept., 1 & 29 Oct. and 12 Nov. 1785
5. LNJ 19 Nov. 1785 and 14 Jan. 1786; LSM 16 Dec. 1785
6. LNJ 29 Oct., 19 & 26 Nov., 3, 10 & 24 Dec. 1785 and 14 Jan. 1786
7. LNJ 30 Nov. 1785, 28 Jan. and 11 Feb. 1786
8. LNJ 4 March 1786
9. LNJ 11 March, 8 & 15 April, and 13 & 20 May 1786
10. LJ 30 Jan., 13 & 27 Feb., 6 & 13 March and 3 & 10 April 1787
11. LJ 22 May 1789
12. LJ 6 Nov. 1789, 2 April, 2, 16 & 30 July and 10 Sept. 1790
13. LJ 31 Dec. 1790, 4 Feb., 11 March, 13 & 20 May 1791

The Act

14. 31 Geo III c 77
15. C. Hadfield & A.W. Skempton: *William Jessop, engineer*. David and Charles, 1979
16. Leicestershire CRO DE336/11A
17. C. Hadfield & A.W. Skempton. *Op. cit.*

Construction
18. LJ 24 June and 8 July 1791; NJ 9 July 1791
19. LJ 8 July 1791
20. Leicestershire CRO DE336/11B
21. D. Goodwin: 'R. Wreake Navigation Notes' (unpublished ms)
22. LJ 9 Sept., 14 Oct., 4 Nov. and 9 Dec. 1791, 2 & 16 March, 6 April & 28 Sept. 1792
23. LSM 7 Dec. 1792, 23 May & 7 Nov. 1794; NJ 8 Nov. 1794
24. LJ 27 March 1795
25. *Leicester Herald* 3 April 1795
26. Share Register, Leicestershire CRO DE336/11B
27. Pocket Diary of Col. John Frewen Turner, East Sussex CRO 744-765
28. Tonnage accounts of Leicester Navigation, Leicestershire CRO
29. 40 Geo III c 55
30. C. Hadfield. *Op. cit.*

Operation
31. LJ 31 Jan. 1794
32. Leicestershire CRO QS 49/1
33. LJ 2 Feb. 1798
34. M.G. Miller: 'Trent Navigation Boat Gauge Tables' (*Journal of the Railway & Canal Historical Society* XXIII, 3 Nov. 1977)
35. D.D. Gladwin: *The Waterways of Britain*
36. LJ 4 Aug. 1797; NJ 10 June 1820 & 17 Jan. 1824
37. T.J. Chandler: 'The Canals of Leicestershire: their development and trade' (*East Midlands Geographer*, No. 10, 1961)
38. C. Hadfield. *Op. cit.*
39. *ibid.*
40. LJ 26 Jan 1816; LJ 2 Feb 1816
41. OS map 25″, XIX 7, 2nd ed. 1903
42. LJ 30 Sept 1808
43. LJ 30 Sept. 1836
44. QS 73/74 1845, Peterborough and Nottingham Jct. Rly.
45. LJ 22 June 1804

The Coming of the Railway, Decline and Closure
46. C. Hadfield. *Op. cit.*
47. The Act authorising the construction of the railway was 9 & 10 Vic c 51; the Act authorising the sale of the canal was 9 & 10 Vic c 255
48. Syston to Peterborough Railway plans, Leicestershire CRO QS 73/32
49. Drury-Lowe Mss, Nottingham University Library, Dr E 134
50. *ibid.* Dr E 134/7
51. Leicestershire CRO 3D42/4/23 item 9
52. 40 & 41 Vic c 78
53. LJ 31 Aug. 1877
54. Leicestershire CRO 3D42/4/23
55. Leicestershire CRO 3D42/4/23 item 10

Conclusion

56.   N. Ashton: *Leicestershire Watermills.* Wymondham: Sycamore Press, c.1977
57.   Severn-Trent Water Authority, Soar Division: 'River Wreake Improvement Scheme'. Leaflet, Sept. 1980

Description

58.   Size of rise at each lock is as given in Bradshaw's map of canals, 1829
59.   Leicester Navigation Papers: Jessop's drawings. Leicestershire CRO 3D42/M37/2/5/6
60.   Bradshaw. *Op. cit.*
61.   C. Hadfield & A.W. Skempton. *Op. cit.*
62.   Severn-Trent Water Authority: Soar Division. *Op. cit.*
63.   Leicestershire CRO 3D42/5/9/3
64.   John Ward: *Chronological events in the history of Melton Mowbray* ... Melton Mowbray: William Loxley, 1889
65.   Melton Navigation Company. Surplus lands at Melton, June 27, 1879. Leicestershire CRO DG25/9/26/19

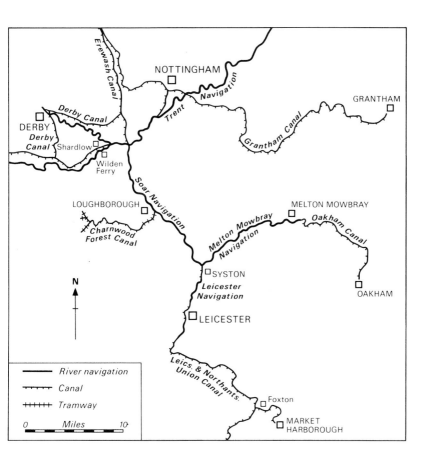

River navigation

Canal

Tramway

0   Miles   10

N

KEY TO STRIP CHARTS

▨	Existing water	▨	Road	
══	Navigation with towing path	──	Footpath	
⅃□⅂	Loop of river	+++++	Railway	
→	Direction of flow	+++++	Railway (disused)	
⌒	By-passed loop of river	⟩─⟨	Bridge	
⌃ ⁄	Lock, Weir	▪ ●	Church (tower/spire)	
*	No significant features visible in this area	▪	Other building	

Broken lines indicate obliterated or fragmentary features

42

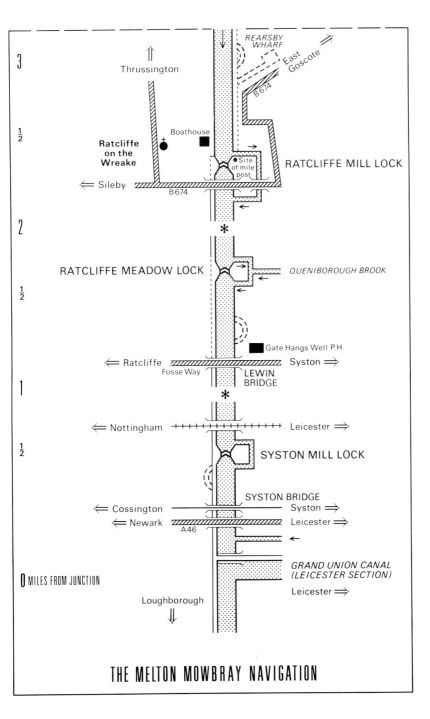

THE MELTON MOWBRAY NAVIGATION

43

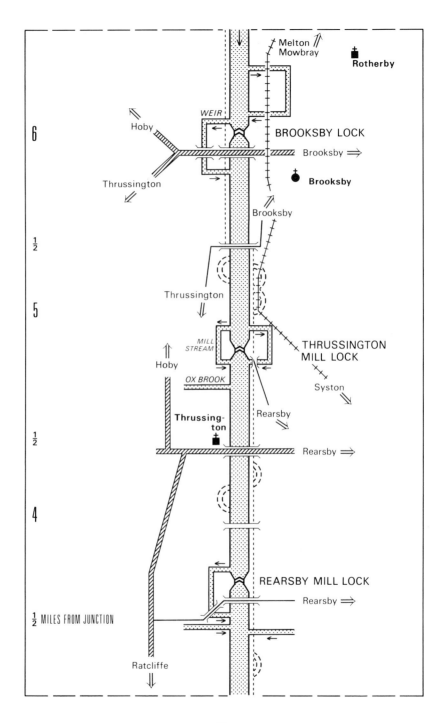

Melton
Mowbray

Rotherby

WEIR

Hoby

BROOKSBY LOCK

6

Brooksby ⟹

Thrussington

Brooksby

½

Brooksby

Thrussington

5

MILL
STREAM

THRUSSINGTON
MILL LOCK

Hoby

Syston

OX BROOK

Thrussing-
ton

Rearsby

½

Rearsby ⟹

4

REARSBY MILL LOCK

Rearsby ⟹

½ MILES FROM JUNCTION

Ratcliffe

44

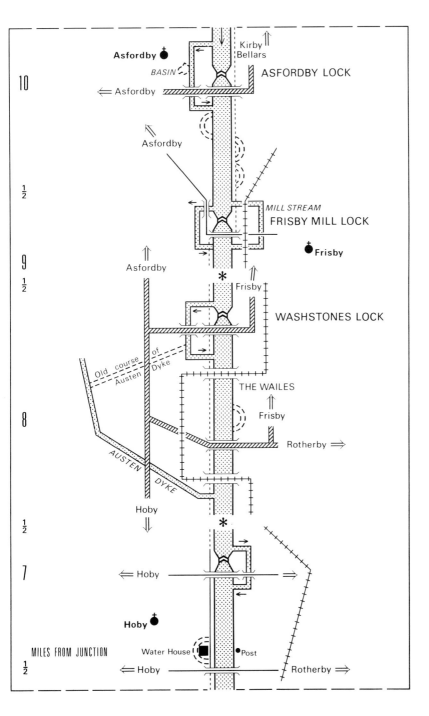

Kirby
Bellars

Asfordby ●

BASIN

ASFORDBY LOCK

10

⟸ Asfordby

Asfordby

½

MILL STREAM

FRISBY MILL LOCK

● Frisby

9

Asfordby

½

*

Frisby

WASHSTONES LOCK

Old course of
Austen Dyke

THE WAILES

Frisby

8

AUSTEN

Rotherby ⟹

DYKE

Hoby

½

*

7

⟸ Hoby

⟹

Hoby ●

MILES FROM JUNCTION

Water House ■ ● Post

½

⟸ Hoby

Rotherby ⟹

45

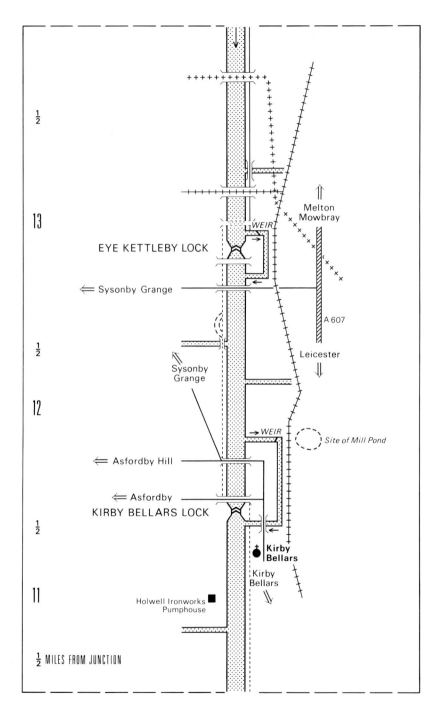

½

13

½ WEIR

EYE KETTLEBY LOCK

⟸ Sysonby Grange

Melton
Mowbray

A 607

Leicester

½

Sysonby
Grange

12

→ WEIR

⟸ Asfordby Hill

⟸ Asfordby

KIRBY BELLARS LOCK

½

Kirby
Bellars

Kirby
Bellars

11

Holwell Ironworks
Pumphouse

◯ Site of Mill Pond

½ MILES FROM JUNCTION

46